The Dad of the Dad of the Dad of your Dad

The Dad of the Dad of the Dad of your Dad

by Jeff Moss

Illustrated by Chris Demarest

BALLANTINE BOOKS • NEW YORK

http://www.randomhouse.com

Library of Congress Cataloging-in-Publication Data
Moss, Jeffrey.
    The dad of the dad of the dad of your dad/by Jeff Moss; illustrated by
Chris Demarest.—1st ed.
        p.   cm.
    Summary: Story poems present adventures of fathers and their sons and
daughters over the centuries from the beginning of time, into the future.
    ISBN 0-345-38591-8
    1. Fathers—Juvenile poetry. 2. Children's poetry, American. 3. Humorous
poetry, American. [1. Fathers—Poetry. 2. American poetry.] I. Demarest,
Chris L., ill. II. Title.
PS3563.088458D34   1996
811'.54—dc20   96-14195

Text design by Roberta Pressel

Manufactured in the United States of America

First Edition: June 1997

10   9   8   7   6   5   4   3   2

For Alex

Contents

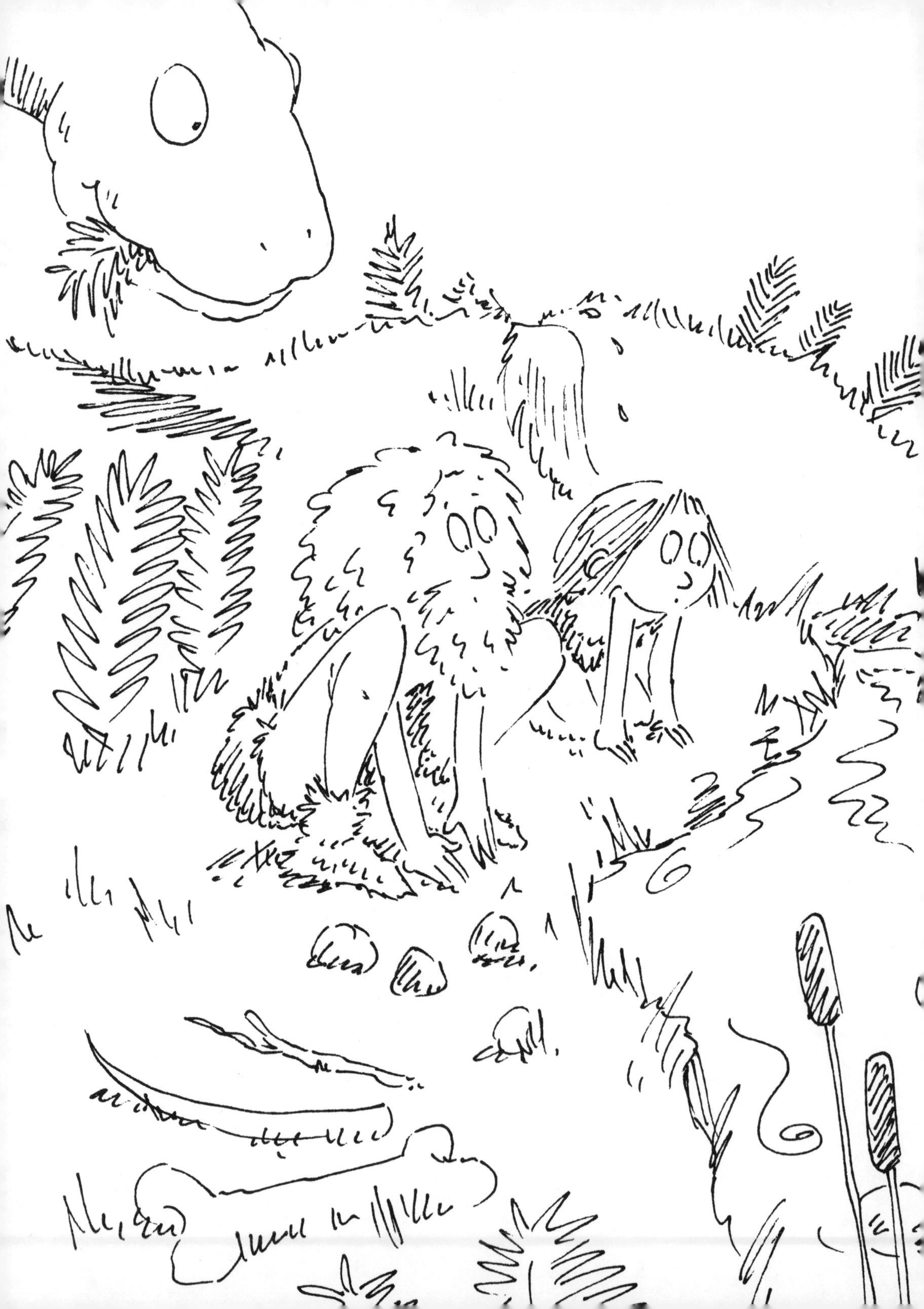

Stones in a Stream

One day, millions of years ago,
As springtime turned the world green,
A boy and a dad took a long quiet walk
And stopped by the side of a stream.
The day was clear and bright and cool,
And nobody else was around.
The whoosh of the water hurrying by
Was the morning's only sound.
The boy and the dad sat still on the grass
And in silence enjoyed the day.
(Of course, back then no one knew how to talk
So there wasn't a lot to say.)
They turned and looked at the blue of the sky
And the white of some dinosaur bones,
Until their eyes fell on some dried-up sticks,
And some different-sized scattered stones.

The dad gazed down. He let out a grunt,
And he moved from his resting place.
With a curious finger, he touched a stone,
And a different look crossed his face.
He turned toward the stream, and his eyes seemed to say
That he wanted to try something more.
And then the dad did a strange new thing
No one ever had done before.

The dad bent over and picked up a stone
And he threw it into the stream.
Then his eyes grew wide as a circle formed
Where the stone pierced the water's gleam.
The boy and the dad stood perfectly still
As they watched the circle grow
Bigger and bigger, till it disappeared
Into dirt-brown banks below.
The dad made a sound—it was not quite a bark
And not quite a hoot of joy.
He bent down and picked up another stone,
And he handed it to the boy.

The boy took the stone and turned toward the stream,
He wanted to try it, too.
And as his dad watched, the boy raised his arm,
And he let out a cry, and he threw.
His head bounced back as he heard the splash,
And then as the circle grew wide,
The boy and dad looked at each other
And they felt something new inside.
There weren't yet words to describe what they felt,
Still somehow, the two of them knew
That in the world, there were special things
That a boy and a dad could do.

All afternoon, by the banks of the stream,
Stones skittered and plopped and skimmed,
One after another, *boom* and *kerplunk*,
As the bright sun slowly dimmed.
Flat stones and round ones, as on and on
They continued, the father and son,
Till a sliver of moon flecked the water,
And, finally, their throwing was done.
They both were happy and tired,
As they quietly stood at rest.
Then slowly the dad wrapped his arms 'round the boy,
And he pulled him close to his chest.
The boy curled his arms around the dad's neck
And they both felt safe and glad,
And that hug became the very first hug
Between a boy and a dad.

A few last throws, then they headed for home,
Full of new things to understand,
As they walked in the light of the thin new moon,
A boy and a dad, hand in hand.

When I Was a Kid

*J*ust before the end of cave-person days,
As people were abandoning their primitive ways,
A girl named Gloog, one night in her cave,
Sat with her father, a man named Dave.
Gloog was in a complaining mood,
She griped about her clothes, her food.
Her stone soup tasted like a terrible mess,
She wanted a new woolly mammoth–skin dress,
She had to keep the fire lit all night long,
Her hieroglyph homework was going all wrong.
She kept complaining how hard things were,
Till her dad sat her down on some animal fur.
Then he cleared his throat and said to her:
"Gloog, you think your life is rough?
Let me tell you when things were *really* tough!

Let me tell you about when *I* was a kid
And all the difficult stuff *I* did.
Now, stop and think how bad you'd feel
If there wasn't any fire to cook a meal.
There was no fire when I was a boy,
Lunch in the Ice Age was hard to enjoy.
Our food would freeze and it wouldn't thaw,
We'd have to eat it cold and raw.
When Mom made a burger, imagine the shock,
It was like biting into ice-cold rock.
Without a fire's warmth or light,
We'd freeze and worry about tigers all night.
(Then, one day, my uncle Bert
Touched something sparkly and cried, 'Ow! That hurt!'
That's how we discovered fire,
And today Uncle Bert is a man to admire.)
Back then, we couldn't grow crops we'd need
'Cause we hadn't yet learned how to plant a seed.
We'd eat grass soup and berries and briar,
And roots that tasted like an old stone tire.

And speaking of tires, how would you feel
If you'd lived before they invented the wheel?
Well, when I was kid, and I cross my heart,
There wasn't one wagon, there wasn't one cart,
Not a single wheel, no skates, no bikes,
We could never take rides, we could only take hikes.

And way back then, we didn't have clothes.
When it rained, we got wet. In the cold, we froze.
No one ever bought a new dress or shirt,
'Cause all we were covered with was lots of dirt.
We had no colored paints at all
To paint pretty animals on the wall.
Back then there were no hieroglyphs
Like the ones we carve in the sides of cliffs
To leave written messages for each other,
Like, 'Mom is out. Take care of your brother.'
We hadn't even learned how to speak,
We sat around grunting week after week.

That's how life was. Well, I've said enough.
Just please don't tell me you've got it rough,
Or any more of that silly stuff,
'Cause when *I* was a kid, it was *really* tough!
Well, Gloog, that's all I have to say!"
"Hmm," thought Gloog, as her dad walked away,
"When Dad was a kid, it's clear to see,
He probably complained as much as me!"

Philomon's Father

*I*n the ancient Greek city of Athens,
In the district where families dwell,
There lived four young ancient Greek children
And their ancient Greek fathers as well.
Now Delia's dad was a soldier,
Leander's dad studied the stars,
Daphne's dad was an athlete....

And Philomon's father made jars.

Daphne said, "My dad's the fastest!
He won the big Marathon race."
"My dad's the bravest!" cried Delia.
"He fought at the battle of Thrace."
Leander said, "My dad is wisest!
He discovered a new bunch of stars."
But the three kids would sometimes tease Philo,
Saying, "Philo's dad only makes jars!"

Now if *your* dad's a famous brave soldier
Or a runner whose speed is the best,
The thought of a jar-making father
May leave you a bit unimpressed.
Still I'll spend a few stanzas describing
Some of Philo's dad's vases and jars.
If you're bored, you can always stop reading
And go off and smoke some cigars.

Philomon's dad was a potter.
He worked at his shop every day,
Making flagons and jars of all sizes
From reddish-brown soft river clay.
He made vases and flasks, jugs and bottles
For water, for oil, and for wine—
Not one was the same as another,
Each had its own shape and design.

Near the door of his workshop stood vases,
Tall and slender as any you've seen,
Calm and quiet, like ladies-in-waiting
To an ancient and elegant queen.
If they spoke, it would be with soft voices,
If they moved, it would be with great grace.
They'd been crafted by Philomon's father
And each held its own special place.

Beside them, lined up at attention
Stood strong-looking urns in a row,
Like warriors, solid and stalwart,
In one single rank, toe-to-toe.
It would take two strong workers to lift one.
To pass, you would have to go 'round.
Philomon's father had shaped them,
And finer urns couldn't be found.

There were round jars with big bulging bellies,
So squat they looked almost like trolls.
Crouched over they seemed to be listening
Through small earlike handles with holes.
Behind them stood tall jars for water,
Like girls with their hands on their hips,
And jars that had gold rims that glistened
When you lifted them close to your lips.

There were urns that were covered with pictures,
They were painted with beauty and skill,
Scenes of markets or chariot races,
Like photographs holding time still.
Deep red or jet black or soft purple
Were the colors you saw everywhere,
All painted by Philomon's father
With hard work and patience and care.

Now one day the kids had teased Philo,
He came to the shop feeling sad.
He said, "Dad, why aren't you famous
Like Leander's or Delia's dad?"
His dad replied, "I'm just a potter,
So I can't be a world-famous man.
Still I'm proud that I make jars and vases,
And to make them the best that I can."

Delia's dad was a soldier,
But today no one's heard of his name.
Daphne's dad was a world-famous athlete,
But it's two thousand years since his fame.
Yet today if you happen to travel
To a large city far from your home,
If you visit the greatest museums
In New York or London or Rome . . .

21

You'll see, safely locked in glass cases,
Things whose beauty has lasted through time,
Though the bright colors now may be faded
And the painted scenes long past their prime.
There they are, though their handles are broken,
There they are and the world can still know
The jars made by Philomon's father,
In his shop, such a long time ago.

Eleanor

Once upon a time, in days of yore
(Many many years ago, or slightly more)
In a simple stone castle on a distant shore,
There lived a young girl named Eleanor.
And this is the story of how Eleanor
Got a bump on her head from the top of a door.

Young Eleanor lived in Throppingham Shire,
Fourth castle down from the church with the spire.
She had three brothers of various ages
Who wanted to be sorcerers or archers or pages.
Their names were Fitzroy and Roderick and Hugh,
And they did the things brothers usually do.
They raced and yahooed through the medieval halls,
They played with their medieval bats and balls,
And they teased their sister in a medieval way,
Pretty much the same as brothers today.
They'd pull Ellie's wimple or call her a name,
Or not let her play in some dumb boys' game.

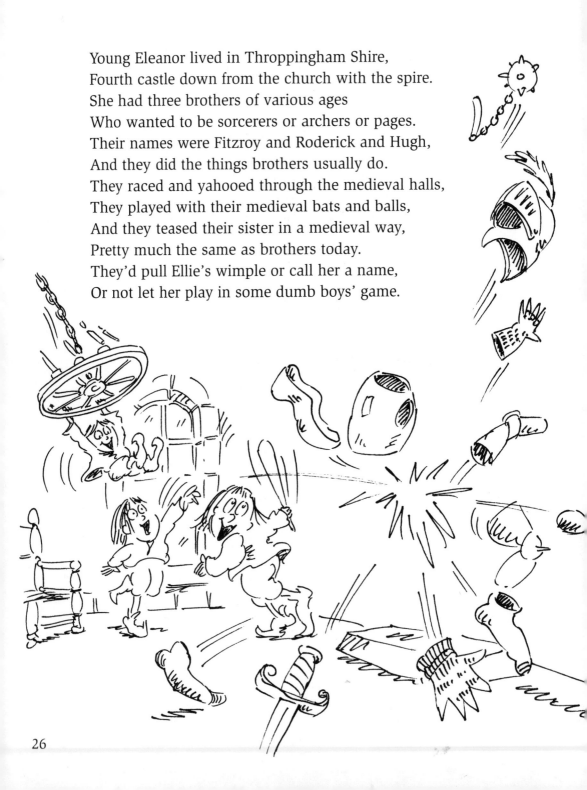

Since things got annoying with that kind of brother,
Occasionally Ellie needed help from her mother.
Eleanor's mother was named Lady Jean,
She taught her to read and to keep her room clean,
And how to play music and weave at a loom,
And she told Ellie's brothers to go to their room.
Ellie loved Jean the way daughters love mothers,
And, most of the time, she got on with her brothers,
But from the time she was very small,
There was someone she liked being with best of all.

Eleanor's father was named Sir Dwight,
He worked all day as a royal knight.
Each morning, after breakfast at the big oak table,
Sir Dwight and Ellie would go to the stable.
They'd saddle his horse, with the help of a groom,
She'd hand him his helmet with the purple plume.
He would wave good-bye, then off he'd ride
Chasing fire-breathing dragons from the countryside.
(In those days, dragons' breath ruined the crops.
They barged through cities and crashed through shops
Destroying all the merchandise before they were through.
So Sir Dwight chased dragons from the cityside, too.)

Now, you get pretty tired by the end of a day
When your job is full of dragons to slay,
And yet Sir Dwight loved nothing more
Than his evening time with Eleanor.
He might tell the story of a dragon he'd slayed,
Or listen to her psaltery as Ellie played.
(In case you don't know what psalteries are,
They're kind of a cross between a harp and a guitar.)
On weekends, she'd help her dad polish his armor,
Or check out the safety of some neighboring farmer.

But of all the things Ellie loved to do,
Her favorite one began when she was just two.
One Saturday morning, at the side of the moat,
After helping Roderick sail his toy boat,
Sir Dwight decided to visit a vassal
Who'd been having dragon trouble on a farm near the castle.
Sir Dwight turned to Ellie and cried, "Onward, ho!"
(That's medieval language for, "Come on, let's go!")
With a swoop, he bent down and reached toward the ground,
He grasped Ellie firmly and turned her around.
Then so quickly she didn't have time to prepare,
He whisked his small daughter straight into the air.
Ellie's heart jumped as he held her up high,
With his arms stretching tall toward the unclouded sky.
She peered at the ground from high over her dad,
A little bit frightened, but giddy and glad.
Then, gently, he lowered her, steady and sure
Till she sat on his shoulders, safe and secure.
With her hands 'round his neck, and one leg on each side,
Off Ellie went, on her first shoulder ride.
They marched toward the vassal's farm humming a song.
Both Sir Dwight and Ellie felt tall and strong,
And later that morning without any hassle,
They conquered the dragon who'd bothered the vassal.

From that day onward, both upstairs and down,
Through green country meadows and streets of the town,
Through summertime heat and through winters much colder,
She rode on her dad with a leg 'round each shoulder.
At the age of just three, on a busy town street,
As the knight tipped his visor to people they'd meet,
The townsfolk would joke with young Eleanor,
Saying, "Haven't I seen that tall person before?
Can that be young Ellie? No, that can't be right.
She's taller by far than her father, Sir Dwight!"

Then the townsfolk would laugh and they'd chuckle a lot.
(Sometimes grown-ups are funny and sometimes they're not.)
But high off the ground, Ellie felt so tall
That she never minded the joking at all.
When Ellie was six, she had grown a bit more,
Her head now reached higher than it had before.
She had to be careful, when off they'd march,
To duck when they went through a doorway or arch.
But though she had grown a bit taller and older,
She still loved to ride with a leg 'round each shoulder.

When Ellie was eight, she set out with her dad
On the bravest adventure that they'd ever had.
They had heard of a dragon so nasty and mean,
He was twice as obnoxious as any you've seen,
Breathing twice as much fire and twice as much smoke,
Smelling two times as smelly, making everyone choke,
With a roar twice as loud and teeth twice as scary
As dragons you'd meet who are just ordinary.
He scared children doubly as they lay in their beds,

And the reason was simple...

He had two heads!

Many strong knights in vain had tried
To chase this beast from the countryside.
Some came home with their armor burned,
Alas, several brave ones never returned.
Sir Dwight packed all the supplies they'd need—
Swords and armor and a book to read.
For Ellie, he packed a helmet and lance,
Some changes of socks and some warm woolen pants.
With food in a barrel and water in a flagon,
They set out to conquer the two-headed dragon.
They rode for ten days and eleven nights,
Through valleys' depths and mountains' heights,
Till, near the desert of Mozandor,
They finally found what they'd been looking for.
Suddenly, dragon-smoke filled the air,
And the foulest smell was everywhere.
Ellie held her nose and cried, "Eeeeyuuu!
It's the smell of a dragon's breath—times two!"
At once, they heard a deafening roar.
Sir Dwight held tight to Eleanor.
"Listen, I can hear him!" she anxiously said.
"Yonder lurks the beast with the extra head!"
Sir Dwight steered their horse behind a large boulder,
And hoisted his daughter high onto his shoulder.
She was wearing her armor and her helmet, too.
"Okay," her dad whispered, "you know what to do!"
They took a deep breath and let out a cry
That echoed far into the darkening sky.

Then, bravely they galloped, Sir Dwight and young Ellie,
Toward the dragon whose breath was so horribly smelly.
The fierce dragon turned as he saw them coming,
The sound of his rumble was like giants drumming.
He snorted and gurgled with a fiery smell,
From deep in her tummy, Ellie wanted to yell.
But before she could utter another word,
Something mysterious and strange occurred.
As he gazed at the galloping knight and maid,
Suddenly, the dragon seemed very afraid.
A terrified look crossed all four of his eyes,
From both of his mouths came two great sighs,

A shudder ran from his heads to his tail,
A shiver swept over each slimy scale.
And amidst all the noise and fire and smoke,
The two-headed dragon trembled and spoke.
As he saw Ellie perched on the shoulders of Dwight,
He howled, "Oh, no, it's a two-headed knight!"
Well, as you can guess, for a two-headed beast,
A two-headed knight is the thing he likes least.
So with both heads hung low, he slunk away.
"We did it!" cried Ellie. Sir Dwight cried "Hooray!"
They never again heard the two-headed roar
And the dragon didn't bother them anymore.

Now the time's bound to come, as a person gets older,
When she's too big to ride on anyone's shoulder.
You might get too heavy, you might grow too tall,
You might lose your balance or take a bad fall.
But though Ellie grew and by now was thirteen,
Her rides on Dwight's shoulders still often were seen,
Till one Tuesday in May when her brother Fitzroy
Came home from school with another boy.
The boy's name was Guy, he was funny and smart,
With red hair and freckles and a very kind heart.
And although he was mostly a friend of her brother,
Still Guy and Ellie liked one another.
Now for this Tuesday's dinner, Ellie was late,
She rode Sir Dwight's shoulders in a most anxious state.
They sped up the stairs at a very great speed,
Sir Dwight almost slipped, Ellie shouted, "Take heed!"
They made a quick left toward the grand dining hall,
Then a right at the unicorn rug on the wall,
And Ellie saw Guy at the table inside . . .
And then came the end of her last shoulder ride.
Ellie wasn't thinking of where she was going,
Ellie wasn't thinking of how she'd been growing.
All she was thinking of was saying "Hi,"
Or something else clever to Fitzroy's friend Guy.

And so, as they rushed through the dining room door,
Something bad happened to Eleanor,
A stroke of the very worst kind of luck—
As she passed through the doorway, she forgot to duck.
The sound that her head made was more than a *clunk*,
It was more like a *bonk*, or a loud *thud* or *thunk*.
Ellie cried "Oof!" and Ellie cried "Oh!"
And a sorrowful "Ow!" and the saddest "Oh, no!"
Her tears started streaming, she choked and she sobbed,
Her head stung and smarted, it ached and it throbbed.
Her brothers all winced and said, "Ooh, what an ouch!"
Sir Dwight carried her to a soft nearby couch.

Her mother and brothers and Guy and her dad
All gathered to see what poor Eleanor had.
What Eleanor had was a very large lump,
What Eleanor had was a very bad bump.
With delicate fingers she reached up and felt
A sensitive, painful, and large egg-sized welt.
They put her to bed and called a physician
Who advised her to rest in a sitting position.
And from that day onward, young Eleanor
Didn't go for shoulder rides anymore.

As time passed and Eleanor grew,
She and her dad found new things to do.
They still loved each other and, besides,
It was past the time for shoulder rides.

Years went by, and then some more,
Till, in another castle on another shore,
Sir Dwight came to visit Guy and Eleanor—
They gave their sons shoulder rides across the floor,
And Sir Dwight told the story of how years before
Ellie bumped her head on the top of a door,
Once upon a time, in days of yore.

The Explorer

rancisco di Morra, the well-known explorer,
Set sail in the summer of 1503.
He left his two children, young Marco and Flora,
At home with their mom, then he set out to sea.

Francisco di Morra, the daring explorer,
Returned in the autumn of 1504
With strange coins for Marco and bright cloth for Flora,
And tales of new lands he had found to explore.

He brought back rare spices from far Bora Bora,
He brought back a purple-striped tiger alive.
Soon, much of the world knew of Signore di Morra,
The best-known explorer of 1505.

The Grand Duchess summoned him to the piazza.
She said, "Listen well to what I have to say—
Great wealth and great fame are two things you'll have lotsa!
Get back to your ship! Explore more right away!"

Di Morra replied, "I am sorry, Signora,
But somehow the order of things seems reversed.
Though one day I'll head back to far Bora Bora,
There's other exploring I have to do first."

Francisco went home to young Marco and Flora,
And planned for a trip to a much nearer shore.
"Come, children," he said, "it's now time to explore a
Small bit of the world right outside our front door."

With Flora, he visited streams of bright water,
The ponds full of lilies, the lakes fresh and cold.
They roamed through the hillsides, the father and daughter,
With each day as rare as explorer's found gold.

With Marco, he studied the night sky's dark aura,
As father and son sat alone 'neath the stars,
Exploring the rich colors of the aurora,
Observing the glow of the red planet Mars.

The seasons passed by till Francisco di Morra
Knew it was time to go traveling once more.
So he hired a crew for his brave ship, *The Dora*,
And once again sailed toward a far distant shore.

Asleep 'neath the deep skies of far Bora Bora,
With pale-shining stars above dark-flowing streams,
Francisco di Morra, the famous explorer,
Saw Marco and Flora in faraway dreams.

Years later, an eager young student named Laura
Asked Marco and Flora about their old dad.
The two would explain that Francisco di Morra
Was one of the best dads a kid ever had—

They'd forgotten the tiger from far Bora Bora,
They only remembered the streams and the stars.
And they said of their father, Francisco di Morra,
"There was no dad-explorer as splendid as ours."

Moving—1622

Imagine it's the year 1622—
Your dad comes home and says to you:
"I've got a new job and we have to move.
I really hope you kids approve."
"Where are we moving to?" you say.
Dad says, "Actually it's quite far away."
Your forehead wrinkles in a frown.
"You mean we're moving to a different town?"
Dad answers, "Hmmm. Well, actually,
We'll be sailing to a new world across the sea.
It's called America or something like that.
I'm afraid it's too far to bring your pet cat."
"Across the sea!" you hear yourself yell.
"Oh, no! Oh, please! Oh, yucch! Oh, smell!
We'll be moving to a world we don't even know—
They only discovered it a few years ago!
Oh, Dad, this is awful! Dad, it's the worst!"
Dad says, "We're sailing on the twenty-first."
You see your friends and you say good-bye.
You hug your cat and you start to cry,
And even Mom is a little sad.
She says, "We have to do it for the family and Dad."
You give your cat to the kid next door
Who you don't even like, so it hurts even more.

Then the ship sets sail and things go wrong.
The waves are rough and the winds are strong,
And your stomach is seasick the whole trip long,
And your meals won't stay down where meals belong.

You sail for a month till, what a shock,
You finally bump into Plymouth Rock,
And you put your feet on solid ground.
You take a deep breath and look around.

Well, there isn't a single person in sight,
Just forest to the left and forest to the right.
In fact there isn't even a street
Or a school to go to or kids to meet.
In fact there isn't even a house,
So you gripe and groan and grumble and grouse,
"Where is my street and where is my city?
Where is my house and where is my kitty?"
You've never felt so all alone.
Dad says, "We'll build a home of our own."
He builds a cabin of logs and mud,
It's fine till it rains, then look out for a flood.
And instead of a kitten, what does Dad get?
A squawking wild turkey to be your new pet!
So . . . if moving makes *your* heart feel sad,
Don't get angry at poor old Dad.
Instead, think of what might happen to you
If you lived back in 1622.

59

The Story of Jesse and the Boots

In the old Wild West lived Cowboy Dan,
A ridin' ropin' kind of man,
With a ten-gallon hat and a big leather saddle,
And a rope he could spin and a horse he could straddle,
And a pair of the finest cowboy boots—
They were sure good-looking—those boots were beauts.
Dan also had a little son.
His name was Jesse and from day one,
What Jesse loved best wasn't games or toys
Or ropes or spurs like other boys,
Not a duck that squeaks, or a train that toots.
Nope, what Jesse loved best was his dad's big boots.

When Jesse was two, just a young galoot,
He first grabbed hold of his dad's big boot.
It was too big to wear, so what did he do?
He put it in his mouth and started to chew.
Well, you don't have to go to cowboy school
To know that boot-chewing makes you drool.
His dad spied Jesse with the boot
And he almost jumped out of his cowboy suit.
He cried, "Hey, whoa there, little Jess!
You're making my boot a slobbery mess!"
And Jesse's dad took the boot away,
'Cause he needed to wear it on roundup day.

On a rainy morning, when Jesse was four,
He saw the boots lying on the floor.
He pulled them on, but because of their size,
They almost came up to the tops of his eyes.
He waddled to the door and hurried outside
To meet his dad coming home from a ride.
But the boots were so big Jesse slipped in the mud,
He fell with a *squish* and a *squoosh* and a *thud*.
There was wet gooey mud all over the place,
In his pants and belly button, ears and face.
His dad rode up crying, "Whoa there, Jess!
You and my boots are a muddy mess!"
And Jesse's dad took the boots away
'Cause he needed to wear them on roundup day.

Jesse got a pony when he was nine,
But his dad's big boots still were on his mind.
He knew the boots were too big for a kid,
Still he wanted to wear them, so here's what he did.
To make them fit, he stuffed paper inside.
Then he jumped on his pony and went for a ride.
But even with paper, the boots still were loose,
Jesse fell from his saddle and banged his caboose.
His dad rode up. "Are you okay, Jesse?
By the way, your feet look pretty messy."
And once more Dan took the boots away
'Cause he needed to wear them on roundup day.

Jesse turned thirteen, he still loved the boots,
And just as sure as an arrow shoots,
One day he saw them near his dad's big chair,
And of course he couldn't leave them there.
So he pulled them on and, mark my word,
Something entirely different occurred.
Somehow the boots weren't loose or tight—
Jesse had grown, the boots fit just right!
They looked so fine, so handsome and dressy,
It was almost as if they'd been made for Jesse.
He looked in the mirror and grinned a big grin,
And just at that moment, his dad walked in.

"Why look at you, Jesse!" cried Cowboy Dan.
"You've sure grown up! You're a fine young man!
Those boots are yours from this day on.
Let's head for the roundup before the day's gone!"
Well, you can imagine how proud Jesse felt.
He hitched up his fancy cowboy belt,
He clamped on his big ten-gallon hat,
And he yelled, "Ti-yippee!" (or something like that).
Then Jesse and his dad rode off in the sun.
That's a pretty sure sign that this story is done.

If Little Red Riding Hood . . .

If Little Red Riding Hood had a dad,
Perhaps things wouldn't have turned out so bad.
He'd have taught her the useful things a dad can teach you,
Like the difference between Grandma and a wolf who'll eat you.
He'd have brought her two photographs to let her see
How completely different two things can be.
He'd show her a picture of his kindly old mother,
And say, "Grandma's one thing. A wolf is another.
Grandma wants to hug you and give you a kiss.
A wolf wants to eat you, and he looks like this—
Big teeth, big ears, and plenty of fur.
Now look at your grandma, does a wolf look like her?
Your report card was great, I know you're smart,
So it shouldn't be hard to tell them apart.
Now, please get to Grandma's before it gets dark,
Don't go through the forest, stay out of the park,
Don't stop to talk to any wolves you meet,
And don't wear that red thing when you walk down the street."

To all this, Red would roll her eyes,
She'd say, "Oh, Daddy, don't you realize
You don't have to worry the least about me?
I'm just as responsible as I can be.
I'll buy some flowers at the Maple Street Florist,
I'll take the short cut through the park and the forest
'Cause it's quicker that way and I'll be good,
And I'll just wear my little red riding hood!"
Since these words were not what he wanted to hear,
Her dad would say, "Hold on a minute, please, dear.
On second thought, Grandma's is pretty far.
Grab the keys from the hook, we'll take the car."
So they'd drive out to Grandma's, just Dad and Red,
And Grandma, when they got there, would be in bed.

"What big lips you have, Grandma!" Red would say with fear.
"All the better," would say Grandma, "to kiss you, my dear!"
Then a bad thing would happen, and it's simply this:
Red would get smacked with Grandma's huge juicy kiss.
Compared to being eaten, that's not so bad . . .
So what a shame Red Riding Hood didn't have a dad!

Mc Fuzz & Sons

In the year thirteen thousand six hundred and eight,
Lived a father much greater than greater-than-great.
He was not just a dad, but a grandfather, too.
He lived on the planet of Outer Kwandu,
Where the average age of the people alive
Was somewhere approaching three hundred and five.
This story concerns a big party he had,
But first, let me tell you about this great dad.
The name of our hero was Henry Mc Fuzz,
And I'd like to explain just how great Henry was.
Though writing it down is a bit of a bother,
Mc Fuzz was a *great-great-great-great-great*-grandfather,
Which, simply put, means that Mc Fuzz had a son,
And that son grew up and then he, too, had one,
And when *that* boy grew up, a young son's what *he* had,
And then *that* son grew up and became a new dad
With a son of his own and before *he* was through,
You guessed it, that son had a son, fine and new,
And then *that* son had *his* son and then, one bright morn,
What else would occur but that *his* son was born?
And of course *this* boy was . . . (and now we are done),
Mc Fuzz's dear *great-great-great-great-great*-grandson.
The boy was named Henry Mc Fuzz Number Eight,
In honor of Henry the greater-than-great.
(In fact, all the sons were named Henry, it's true—
Numbers Seven, Six, Five, Numbers Four, Three, and Two.)

Now, each Hank Mc Fuzz had a self all his own,
From the time he was young through the time he was grown.
One was short, one was tall, one was stern, one was funny,
One loved the Ice Planets, one loved hot and sunny.

Some ate red spaghetti from
   the planet Oofeetza,
And some liked their food pills
   to taste like cold pizza.

One worked as a korf, one worked as a cook,
And one wrote an intergalactic math book.

But though all were different, still all shared a name,
And one more Mc Fuzz thing was always the same.
For every Mc Fuzz that the world ever knew,
Wherever he'd go and whatever he'd do,
One thing forever was truer than true:
Mc Fuzz family space helmets *always* were blue.
It wasn't that anyone told them, "You've got to!"
It's just that it seemed very un–Mc Fuzz not to.
They never wore green, they never wore red.
You'd never see purple on one Mc Fuzz head.
Just blue as the ocean and blue as the sky,
They all wore blue helmets, though no one knew why.
All they knew was this habit had long since begun
Six hundred years past, when Mc Fuzz Number One
Got helmets of blue for himself and his son.
Then the custom had passed down to each Mc Fuzz lad,
From their favorite *great-great-great-great-great-*granddad.

Now, among all the Henrys, from One up to Eight,
I must tell of a friendship much greater than great—
The friendship between old Mc Fuzz Number One
And young Henry, his *great-great-great-great-great*-grandson.
The two would read books, or play games, or just talk,
Or put on their helmets and go for a walk,
Or watch spaceball games on the wall-to-wall screen,
Or work at young Hank's homework-pumping machine.
And nothing but good times was all that they had,
This boy and his *great-great-great-great-great*-granddad.
The two were like best pals, that's just how it was
With the oldest and youngest Henry Mc Fuzz.

Now . . . about the big party I mentioned before,
It's time to explain just a little bit more.
Since all the Mc Fuzzes lived far from each other,
They'd sometimes feel sad and would miss one another.
So once, each galactical solar light-year,
Throughout the universe, there would appear
In each Mc Fuzz mailbox in all the space nations,
Elegant handmade Mc Fuzz invitations:

Come to the Party,
in Fair or Foul Weather,
It's Time for Mc Fuzzes
to Gather Together!

Yes, once every light-year, a party was had
Where every Mc Fuzz kid, and each mom and dad
Would play games and sing songs, have fun and give thanks,
At a large birthday party for one of the Hanks.
This year, the birthday they'd all celebrate
Was that of the youngest Mc Fuzz, Number Eight.
The party would be held with great ballyhoo,
At his very great-granddad's on Outer Kwandu.
Now you can imagine old Henry Mc Fuzz,
How happy and proud and excited he was
To have a big party where he was the host,
For the birthday of one of the ones he loved most.

He called for a space-taxi six days before,
Rode twelve thousand miles to the space station store
And purchased a present for young Henry Eight,
With a card: "For a boy who's *great-great-great-great-great!*"
Five nights later, the Endor moons rose, bright as flame.
Then they fizzled and sank. Then the party day came!
Well, on every known thing you could ride, steer, or drive,
Mc Fuzz family members began to arrive.
They came by space schooner with green laser sails,
They whirred in by jet train on fiber-thin rails.
Some rode on the back of a six-toed gazork,
One flew in a space-cab from Brooklyn, New York.
By subsonic beamers and light-wave transporters,
From nearby pink moons, and from far-distant quarters,
Blue Mc Fuzz helmets all whizzed through the air,
Till just about all the Mc Fuzzes were there.
At last, proudly sitting behind the fifth wheel
Of a shiny new self-steering quadromobile,
Came Henry Mc Fuzz Numbers Seven and Eight,
The young birthday boy and his dad, a bit late.

And every Mc Fuzz child and woman and man
Cried, "Hurrah, yay, Mc Fuzz!" and the party began!
You wouldn't believe all the games that they played—
Air tennis, space hockey, starship parade,
Hide-and-blast-off, pin the tail on the zerkle,
A race on gazork-back around a large circle.
Last they played spaceball and young Hank hit one
Nine hundred miles, past the pale Uxor sun.
He ran for twelve bases, a Kwandu home run!

Just then, the huge clock on the Great Field of Green
Gonged and *kabonged* as it struck seventeen,
And everyone knew as they heard the bells peal,
The time had now come for the Big Birthday Meal.
It's hard to describe just which food was the best,
There were so many wonderful things to ingest.
There were pickles from Pluto as hard as a brick,
There were cold dogs with mustard, ice-stiff on a stick.
There were burgers from Booglia covered with firth,
And French fries from France on the small planet Earth.
For dessert, Hank's Aunt Brutha had found time to bake
A huger-than-huge upside-down birthday cake.
So they sang, "Happy birthday, dear Henry, to you!"
In English and Martian and Snurf and Kwandu.

Then, at last, it was time for Mc Fuzz Number Eight
To open his presents. Young Hank couldn't wait.
All of the Henrys moved up close to see,
As he opened the gifts from his large family.
First, a mystery board game from First Cousin Janet
Called, *Who Did That Crime and with What on Which Planet?*
Then some cool antigravity basketball shoes,
And a touch-and-sing disc called *Green Slime Sings the Blues*,
And some di-thermal, all-weather long underwear—
Then a large, unmarked box that was simple and square.
Henry lifted the lid and peeked slowly inside . . .

"Look at this!" Henry whispered, "Oh, no!" someone cried.
"You can't have that present! Tsk, tsk, and tut-tut!"
It was Henry's dad speaking. He slammed the lid shut.
Then the rest of the Henrys all peeked inside, too,
And they strongly agreed with Hank's dad's point of view.
Number Six said, "Bad present, by golly, gee whiz!
My dad didn't have one and neither did *his*."
 "Of course not!" said Five. "For if you're a Mc Fuzz,
That's surely a something that nobody does."
Then Four turned to *his* dad and said to Hank Three,
"That gift is no present that you'd get from me."
"Not ever!" said Three. "That gift simply won't do."
"Who'd *give* it? Not I!" cried Mc Fuzz Number Two.
Then all of the Henrys turned toward each other
With all the same questions to ask one another.
"Who'd ever give *that* gift to *any* Mc Fuzz?
It's the strangest Mc Fuzz present there ever was!
Where did it come from, and how could it be . . . ?"
Then there was silence. And then, quietly,
A familiar voice answered, "Ahem . . . It's from me."

Heads spun to see where the voice had come from.
Jaws dropped and throats gasped, Mc Fuzzes stood numb.
For they looked and they saw and they knew the voice was
The voice of old Number One Henry Mc Fuzz.
"It only seems natural to try a small change,"
Old Henry continued. "It doesn't seem strange."
"Not strange?" cried the others. "For eight generations,
We've had not one change! We've had no deviations!
It started when *your* son was only a lad,
And now you're a *great-great-great-great-great*-granddad!"

Each Henry stood silent, from Seven through Two,
Not one confused Henry knew quite what to do,
Till, finally, young Henry Mc Fuzz Number Eight
Stepped up to his Grandpa, the Greater-Than-Great.
The question he needed to ask was so large,
It was huge as a whale and as broad as a barge.
Some Mc Fuzzes were dizzy, some felt indigestion,
Awaiting the answer to such a big question.
And now you will hear what the big question was
That was asked by young Hank to old Henry Mc Fuzz.
He said, "Mc Fuzz helmets are blue as the sky.
What we want to ask you, Great-Grandpa, is: *Why?*"

Henry the First stood there, kindly and wise,
A faraway memory clouded his eyes.
Then Henry Mc Fuzz the First quietly said,
"I'm not sure why they're blue. They could have been red.
Or they could have been pink, if you know what I mean.
They could have been purple, they could have been green.
But they only had blue at the space helmet store,
On that day in the year thirteen thousand and four,
So I just got some blue ones. That's all, nothing more."
A murmuring sound, like a thousand bee buzzes,
Swirled and whirled over the many Mc Fuzzes.
"He just picked a blue one, that's all, nothing more!
It's the color they had at the space helmet store!"

With their thoughts in a jumble, their minds in a haze,
Mc Fuzzes sat muddled, and deep in a daze
As they pondered the present that Henry had got.
They had to do something, but no one knew what.
Till, at last, can you guess what young Henry did?
He opened the present, he took off the lid.
And from out of the box, up onto his head,
Came a brand-new space helmet, a bright shiny red!

"That's from me," smiled old Henry. "It happened again,
Just the same kind of way that it happened back then.
I wanted a helmet. They only had red.
So I thought, 'Well, I'll get him a red one instead!' "
Again, like the whirr of a thousand bee buzzes,
A strange new sensation swept through the Mc Fuzzes.

It touched everyone in the cool evening air,
And a wonderful thing happened right then and there:
Every Mc Fuzz somehow knew right away,
Yes, each Mc Fuzz knew now . . . that *red* was okay.

A great cheer sprang up, "Yay, Mc Fuzz, hip, hooray!
Mc Fuzz, hip-hip, Fuzz, hip-hip, Fuzz, hip, hooray!"
Then, the great Mc Fuzz party went on, on, and on,
Till the light of the six moons of Endor was gone.

From that moment onward, the family Mc Fuzz
Did what most every other space family does.
Some Mc Fuzzes wore green helmets, some would wear red,
Some wore pale yellow or orange instead.
Each Mc Fuzz wore a helmet, no matter the color,
Some a bit brighter and some a bit duller.
It wasn't that anyone told them, "You've got to!"
It just no longer seemed very un–Mc Fuzz not to.

But . . .

Once every light-year, the time always came
When Mc Fuzzes wore helmets that all were the same.
For they sat down and thought and they figured it out—
Just what wearing blue helmets was *really* about.
Now, at every big party, each light-year or two,
Mc Fuzzes know why they wear helmets of blue.
Mc Fuzzes have learned it can make you feel glad,
If you're *any* grown father or *any* young lad,
To do the same thing that your father once had,
Or the dad of the dad of the dad of your dad!
So, that's how it is, and that's how it was,
For each and for all of the Family Mc Fuzz.
And possibly that's how it always will be,
For every Mc Fuzz, and for you, and for me.